JOHN WESLEY POWELL

Soldier, Scientist, and Explorer

CHARLES W.
MAYNARD

The Rosen Publishing Group's

PowerKids Press™

New York

For National Park Service friends who look after America's treasures

"We have an unknown distance yet to run, an unknown river to explore. What falls there are, we know not; what rocks beset the channel, we know not; what walls ride over the river, we know not."
—John Wesley Powell, August 13, 1869, journal entry

Published in 2003 by The Rosen Publishing Group, Inc.
29 East 21st Street, New York, NY 10010

First Edition

Managing Editor: Kathy Kuhtz Campbell
Book Design: Maria E. Melendez

Photo Credits: Cover and title page © National Portrait Gallery, Smithsonian Institution/Art Resource; pp. 4, 20 © Bettmann/CORBIS; pp. 7, 19 Map Division, Library of Congress; pp. 8, 12 (top) Prints and Photographs Division, Library of Congress; pp. 9, 10 courtesy Utah State Historical Society; used with permission of the National Museum of Natural History, S.I.; pp. 11, 12 (bottom), 15, 16 Still Picture Branch, National Archives and Records Administration; p. 22 courtesy U.S. Geological Survey Library, used with permission of the National Museum of Natural History, S.I.

Maynard, Charles W. (Charles William), 1955–
John Wesley Powell, soldier, scientist, and explorer / Charles W. Maynard.— 1st ed.
    p. cm. — (Famous explorers of the American West)
Includes bibliographical references and index.
Summary: A biography of explorer John Wesley Powell, chronicling his life as a soldier and scientist.
  ISBN 0-8239-6290-3
1. Powell, John Wesley, 1834–1902—Juvenile literature. 2. Explorers—West (U.S)—Biography—Juvenile literature. 3. Colorado River (Colo.-Mexico)—Discovery and exploration—Juvenile literature. 4. West (U.S.)—Discovery and exploration—Juvenile literature. 5.Soldiers—United States—Biography—Juvenile literature. 6. Scientists—United States—Biography—Juvenile literature. [1. Powell, John Wesley, 1834–1902. 2. Explorers. 3. Geologists. Colorado River (Colo.–Mexico)—Discovery and exploration. 5. Grand Canyon (Ariz.)—Discovery and exploration. 6. West (U.S.)—Discovery and exploration.] I. Title.
  F788.P88 M39 2003
  550'.92—dc21
                                                                                                                  2001006965

Manufactured in the United States of America

CONTENTS

In this 1873 photo, Powell talks with Tau-gu, a chief of the Southern Paiute, in the Colorado River valley. Powell wanted to understand Native Americans by studying their languages, folktales, and beliefs.

NATURE'S LESSONS

John Wesley Powell was born in Mount Morris, New York, on March 24, 1834. John Wesley was called Wes by his family and was the fourth of Joseph and Mary Powell's six children. The Powells sailed to America from England in 1830. They settled first in New York, where John was born, and then in southern Ohio.

When John was nine years old, he went to live with a family friend, George Crookham, to get an education. Crookham loved to study nature. He collected fossils, rocks, and **artifacts**. He took John on trips through the countryside to collect **specimens**. He taught John to respect all people. He told John about African Americans escaping from slavery, helped by the **Underground Railroad**. Crookham's teachings stayed with John all his life.

Powell enjoyed studying the specimens of rocks, plants, and fossils that he collected on his way down the Mississippi River in the summer of 1856.
He took another river journey in 1857. This time he began in Pittsburgh, Pennsylvania. He rowed down the Ohio and Mississippi Rivers, all the way to the Gulf of Mexico.

In 1846, Powell's family moved to Wisconsin. There was no school near his wilderness home, so Powell walked the 20 miles (32 km) to Janesville, Wisconsin, where he went to school. He loved to study science. He especially liked **geology**, the study of rock types and the formation of Earth. In 1851, after moving to Bonus Prairie, Illinois, he decided to learn more about geology and nature. In the summer of 1855, he walked across Illinois and bought a rowboat. Next he rowed up the Mississippi River to St. Paul, Minnesota. He then walked through Wisconsin and Michigan.

To make a living while he studied, Powell taught in one-room schoolhouses. During summer 1856, he traveled to St. Paul and rowed down the Mississippi River from the Falls of Saint Anthony in Minneapolis, Minnesota, to New Orleans, Louisiana, to collect specimens.

Boats sail down the Mississippi River past Saint Paul, Minnesota. In summer 1856, Powell went to St. Paul to begin his trip down the Mississippi. On his trip, he collected rocks, plants, and fossils to study.

Union troops answer Confederate attacks before retreating on the first day of the Battle of Shiloh. On April 6, 1862, a Confederate bullet hit Captain Powell in the right arm while he fought in this battle.

MILITARY HARDSHIPS

When the **Civil War** began in 1861, Powell joined the Union army. He rose quickly in rank to **captain** of an **artillery** company. In November 1861, Powell took a short leave from his company to marry Emma Dean, whom he had met in Detroit, Michigan, in 1855.

On April 6, 1862, during the Battle of Shiloh in Tennessee, a bullet struck Powell in his right arm. His brother, Walter, who served in the same artillery company, took Captain Powell to the hospital boat that was anchored on a nearby river. Two days later, a doctor cut off Powell's right arm just below the elbow. He returned to the army two months later, but his arm always hurt.

Returning to duty two months after being wounded, Powell later fought in the battles at Vicksburg, Nashville, and Atlanta. He became a major in 1863. Many people called him Major Powell for the rest of his life. He left the army in January 1865.

ROCKY MOUNTAIN ADVENTURES

This photo of Emma Dean Powell was taken around 1869. Emma went with her husband and his group to explore the Rockies in Colorado in 1867. When they climbed Pikes Peak, Emma became one of the first women to reach its top.

After the Civil War ended in 1865, Powell taught geology at Illinois Wesleyan University in Bloomington, Illinois. He later became the **curator** of the museum of the Illinois State Natural History Society. To collect specimens for the museum, Powell led a group of students and friends to the Rocky Mountains in 1867. Emma, Powell's wife, also went with the group. The Powells and their group traveled in the Front Range of the Rocky Mountains.

In summer 1868, the Powells returned to Colorado with about 20 friends and students. They explored the Rockies in search of more museum specimens. They climbed Longs Peak, near Estes Park, which today is a part of Rocky Mountain National Park. The Powells stayed near the White River during the winter. Powell became friends with the **Ute**. He studied their language and tried to make a dictionary of their words.

Powell and others (above) explore the Green River in 1871–1872. While in the Rocky Mountains in 1868, Powell saw part of the Colorado River from Longs Peak and began to plan his first expedition down the river.

Powell is seen here in 1871, standing in the middle boat, at Green River Station, Wyoming. Powell and nine men left from here on their first trip down the Colorado River. That trip started on the Green River on May 24, 1869.

A member of Powell's group sits on a bank of the Green River in 1871–1872. Powell's group on this trip included artists and photographers. After traveling on severe rapids, they would reach stretches of calm waters, such as this one in the Canyon of Lodore in Colorado.

DOWN THE GREEN RIVER

On May 24, 1869, Powell and nine men left Green River Station in Wyoming Territory in four small boats. The small group carried enough supplies to last for more than six months. The boats ran the first rapids on the Green River easily. Powell and his men named the canyons and the rivers as they explored the unfamiliar region. He and some of the men made careful notes about their trip in **journals**. At some rapids, the men lowered the boats along the bank with ropes. At other rapids, they had to **portage** around the rushing water. After only two weeks on the river while in the Canyon of Lodore, one of the boats crashed on the rocks in the rapids. The other men rescued their friends. Valuable supplies and tools either sank or floated away. The men called the place Disaster Falls.

> "We are now ready to start our way down the Great Unknown. Our boats, tied to a common stake, chafe [rub] each other as they are tossed by the fretful river."—*John Wesley Powell, August 13, 1869, journal entry*

Powell's group continued to travel down the Green River. One day Powell climbed a cliff to scout a rapid. He became stuck on a ledge high above the rushing water. He could not hold on long with his one arm. George Bradley climbed above him but could not reach him. Bradley took off his long underwear and lowered it to Powell. He pulled Powell to safety with his long johns.

The group finally reached the Colorado River. Supplies were running low, and food had spoiled. They spent four days drying their supplies and repairing their boats. Then they continued into the "Great Unknown," as Powell called the river. No one had traveled down the Colorado River to explore it. There were no maps of the area. Powell and his group were the first men to go down through the deep canyons of the Colorado River.

Powell's photographer, E. O. Beaman, took this picture of the Colorado River in Glen Canyon during the 1871–1872 survey trip. The original label on the photo reads "Desolation," or wasteland.

This view of the Grand Canyon from Lava Pinnacle is looking downstream. The photo was taken during Powell's second expedition on the Colorado River from 1871 to 1872.

As the men journeyed down the Colorado River, they stayed wet and hungry. Their clothes, blankets, and food never dried. After three months on the Green and Colorado Rivers, the men opened their last sack of flour. Just two days later, on August 27, 1869, they came to a large rapid. George Bradley called it "the darkest day of the trip." The next day, three of the men decided to leave the **expedition**. They believed they would die in the canyon, and that it would be better to walk out. Powell called the place Separation Rapid.

On August 30, Powell's men, in torn clothing, floated out of the Grand Canyon to the Virgin River. They found out later that the other three men had been killed by Shivwits, a band of Paiute, who mistook them for murderers.

MAPPING THE WEST

Powell returned to the Green and Colorado Rivers in 1871 with another expedition. This time, the group **surveyed** and mapped the area. E. O. Beaman, a photographer, went along to record the scenery. Powell redesigned the boats for the second trip. One of the boats had a chair for him to sit on so he could scout the river and give directions to the others. This trip was to last for a year and a half.

Powell left the men on the river several times to meet with Native Americans. He also went to Salt Lake City, Utah, to be with Emma for the birth of their only child, Mary, on September 8, 1871.

Powell directed surveys in Utah, Arizona, Nevada, and Colorado from 1871 to 1879. He also met and studied many Native Americans of the West. He thought it was important to learn the languages and beliefs of these people.

A 1908 map shows explorers' routes down the Green and Colorado Rivers to the Grand Canyon, including Powell's first and second trips. Inset: Powell's map of the Colorado shows the 1872–1873 surveys.

TIMELINE

1834 On March 24, John Wesley Powell is born to Joseph and Mary Powell in Mount Morris, New York.

1838 The Powell family moves from New York to Ohio.

1855 John Wesley Powell makes the first of his many collection trips.

1861 On May 8, he joins the Union army. On November 28, he marries Emma Dean.

1862 On April 6, Powell is wounded at the Battle of Shiloh; his forearm is later cut off.

1865 On January 4, he leaves the army. Powell becomes a professor of geology at Illinois Wesleyan University.

1867 He becomes curator of the museum for the Illinois State Natural History Society.

On June 1, he begins his first scientific expedition to the West.

1868 In June Powell leads another scientific expedition to the West.

1869 From May to August, Powell leads nine men on the first Colorado River trip.

1871 Powell leads a second trip down the Colorado River.
On September 8, Mary, the Powells' daughter, is born.

1875 Powell joins the staff of the U.S. Geological Survey.

1879 Powell is named the first director of the Bureau of Ethnology.

1881 Powell becomes the second director of the U.S. Geological Survey.

1894 On May 4, Powell resigns as director of the U.S. Geological Survey.

1902 On September 3, John Wesley Powell dies at his home in Haven, Maine.

Powell is seen here with a Southern Paiute guide in the Colorado River valley around 1872. Powell studied Native Americans to learn their traditions and languages.

A SCISTIFIC LIFE

John Wesley Powell studied the land and its people his whole life. In 1879, he became the first director of the **Bureau of Ethnology** at the Smithsonian Institution. This department worked to study the Native Americans of the United States. Three years later, Powell became the director of the U.S. Geological Survey, which makes maps of the country. In his work, he used his experiences in the West and his studies in science to help the nation.

On his greatest adventure, in 1869, Powell made a trip down the Green and Colorado Rivers through the Grand Canyon. Besides mapping and studying the land, he studied the Native Americans he met. Powell's goal was to have a better understanding of the land and its people. Powell lived his life for the advancement of science.

John Wesley Powell sits in his office in the Adams Building at the Smithsonian Institution, in Washington, D.C. Powell's legacy continues to inspire geologists and students of Native American languages throughout the United States.

John Wesley Powell overcame his disability and accomplished many great goals. He helped to organize the National Geographic Society in 1888. He was a founding member of the Sierra Club, which was started by John Muir in 1892. Powell's long life ended on September 3, 1902, at his home in Haven, Maine. His work did not end with his death, though. The U.S. Geological Survey still makes maps. Lake Powell, on the Colorado River in Utah, helps people remember his exploring and mapping work. Powell's careful studies of Native Americans continue to be used to better understand the people who first lived in the West.

GLOSSARY

artifacts (AR-tih-fakts) Objects created or produced by humans.

artillery (ar-TIH-luhr-ee) Cannons or other weapons for firing missiles, such as cannonballs.

Bureau of Ethnology (BYUR-oh UV eth-NAH-luh-jee) A part of the Smithsonian Institution that studied Native Americans and their cultures.

captain (KAP-ten) An officer in the armed forces; in an army, a captain ranks below a major.

Civil War (SIH-vul WOR) A war between two sides within one country. America's Civil War was fought in the United States between the Union (northern states) and the Confederates (southern states) from 1861 to 1865.

curator (KYUR-ay-tuhr) A person who is in charge of a museum, a collection, a zoo, or a library.

expedition (ek-spuh-DIH-shun) A trip for a special purpose, such as scientific study.

geology (jee-AH-luh-jee) The study of rocks and the formation of the crust of Earth.

journals (JER-nuhlz) Notebooks in which people write their thoughts and observations.

portage (POR-tij) To carry boats and supplies around a falls or a rapid.

specimens (SPEH-sih-minz) People or things that show what a whole group is like; samples.

surveyed (ser-VAYD) Measured and made the boundaries, positions, and contours of an area.

Underground Railroad (UN-dur-grownd RAYL-rohd) A system set up to help slaves move to freedom in the North.

Ute (YOOT) Native Americans who once lived in Utah, Colorado, and New Mexico.

INDEX

PRIMARY SOURCES

Cover. *John Wesley Powell*. This undated portrait of Powell was painted by Edmund Clarence Messer. Messer, who lived from 1842 to 1919, is known for his portraits and landscapes. **Page 4**. *John Wesley Powell and Tau-gu, a Chief of the Southern Paiute*. This photo was taken by one of Powell's photographers during the second trip down the Colorado River, from 1871 to 1872. **Page 7**. *City of St. Paul*. An 1853 lithograph shows the Mississippi River as it flows by the city of St. Paul, Minnesota. **Page 8**. *Battle of Shiloh*. This scene of the battle was painted around 1888 by artist Thure de Thulstrup. It shows the area of the battle that was located across from Peach Orchard, and it was called the Hornet's Nest, because of the buzzing sounds of all the flying bullets. **Page 10**. *Emma Dean Powell*. This photograph of Powell's wife was taken in Chicago around the year 1869. **Page 11**. *The Green River in the Canyon of Lodore, Colorado*. This photo was taken during Powell's second expedition to the Colorado River. John "Jack" Hillers, the photographer, first joined Powell's group as a teamster. He then assisted Powell's first photographer, E. O. Beaman, who later left the expedition. Hillers, who had fought in the Union army in the Civil War, became a good friend of Powell's and served as chief photographer for the Bureau of Ethnology for many years. **Page 12 (top)**. *The Green River Station, Wyoming Territory*. Powell's 1871–1872 survey group is shown here at the start of their trip. The photographers during this trip included E. O. Beaman, Jack Hillers, and James Fennemore. **Page 12 (bottom)**. *Frederick S. Dellenbaugh Sits on the Bank of the Green River*. Dellenbaugh, an artist and a mapmaker, accompanied Powell on the second expedition down the Colorado, from 1871 to 1872. This scene shows him viewing the Canyon of Lodore. His sketches and maps were among the first depicting this region of the country. Dellenbaugh's Butte, near the Green River, was named for the youngest member of the expedition. **Page 15**. *In Glen Canyon, on the Colorado River*. E. O. Beaman took this photo during Powell's second survey. **Page 16**. *A View of Grand Canyon from Lava Pinnacle*. This photo was taken during Powell's second trip. The small figure of a man sitting at the edge of the right bank might be Walter "Clem" Powell, Powell's cousin, who also assisted the photographers. **Page 19**. *Diagram Showing the History of the Exploration, Navigation, and Survey of the Grand and Other Cañons of the Colorado River of the West from 1540 to 1908*. This 1908 map shows many explorers' expeditions, including Powell's first and second trips, on the Colorado River and in the Grand Canyon. **Page 19 (inset)**. *Preliminary Map No. 2 of the Country Surveyed in 1872 and 1873*. This 1873 map shows Powell's expedition through the Grand Canyon. **Page 20**. *Major Powell and a Paiute Guide in the Colorado River Valley, Around 1872*. Powell studied as many Native American languages and customs as possible during his trips. **Page 22**. *Powell in His Office in the Adams Building on F Street, N.W., in Washington, D.C.* DeLancey Gill took this photo in the 1890s, and it is in the Smithsonian Institution's National Anthropological Archives.

WEB SITES

Due to the changing nature of Internet links, PowerKids Press has developed an online list of Web sites related to the subject of this book. This site is updated regularly. Please use this link to access the list:
www.powerkidslinks.com/feaw/jwpowel/